The Mullet Man Chronicles.

The Oak View Mystery

By Richard Senate

This work is dedicated to loving daughter Megan Senate who first alerted me to Mullet Man and time travel.

I wish to thank the mysterious Mullet Man without whom this book would not be possible. Enjoy your stay in Encino, in the year 1959, you are beyond the reach of your enemies now. Until we meet again.

Ventura, California 2011

CONTENTS

Introduction

I am a Ghost Hunter and I have been one since one July night in 1978 when I saw a ghost with my own eyes. From that time on I have investigated haunted houses all over the world, but I never thought I would get involved with the subject of time travel and those who have journeyed in the forth dimension. I have found that my years of research were, I believe, preparing me for this new quest all along. As I look into the subject of ghosts I can see that many of the events were, in fact, linked more to the fragile nature of time itself rather than some supernatural phenomena.

I should start at the beginning. My father-in-law retired and moved to Carson City, Nevada to enjoy his golden years and for a time he did travel, fish and enjoy bowling until his health declined to a point where he found it harder and harder to get around. My wife, Debbie, moved up to the Carson Valley to help him but he declined slowly. After years of living apart, Debbie in Carson City and I in Ventura, California, I retired from my job of 22 years and joined her. In a little over a year and a half her father passed away. After the funeral Debbie asked that we return to Ventura where we had friends.

Moving back to California was no small feat but, with luck and pluck Debbie and I managed to sell the house in Carson City and make the move. We quickly found that we were unable to find a home in our price range in beach-side Ventura and had to widen our search to Ojai and inland. We needed to find a house and find it soon. That's when we found a home in Oak View. Oak View is a small community of some 5,000. It's a town with out sidewalks, where horses and chickens out number the people. Most wear baseball caps and drive pick-up trucks. It's only a few miles north of Ventura but it might as well be a hundred miles away. It is laid back country living at its best. Oak View is a small town in a forgotten valley. It's a place most drive through without a passing thought. If they stop at all it's to buy some gas as they go fishing or maybe some beer or a steak or two for the grill. In some ways it reminds me of the California I recalled as a kid, so it was easy to fit in. I never suspected that there was something else in Oak View and that this hamlet had strange properties. It is, I believe, a natural time vortex that with some luck one could pierce the veil of time and travel back and forth. I knew the history of the place from my research and I should have guessed it all along.

The first to live here were an unknown people named the Oak Grove People by their discoverer, Archaeologist Bob Browne. He found a rich site on the hills overlooking the valley. Here thousands of early artifacts were discovered. One piece is displayed in the Ojai Museum today. A small statue of a Toad that might well be the oldest sculpture on the North American Continent. Clearly this early Native People saw this as a sacred place. New trends in archeology have re-named the Oak Grove People the Milling Stone Horizon for the stone mortars discovered at their sites. Perhaps these early people felt something odd about the place.

The Spanish Explorers pass though the area as they established their missions. When they did, at a place now called Casitas Springs, they saw a strange shrine erected by the Chumash Native Americans who had replaced to Oak Grove people 3,000 years ago. The shrine was a large tree, bent into an archway. Suspended from the middle of the arch was a wooden statue. It resembled a puppet more than anything else. All around the image were offerings of shell beads and colorful feathers prized by the natives. The natives told them the statue could be moved and when it was, the world would change. They could use this to place curses and see the land of the dead. The Spanish, good Roman Catholics all, saw it as the handy work of Satan, a heathenish idol, and burned it. They replaced the doll with a wooden cross. Not far away, they would build a small branch Mission they named Santa Gertrudis in 1808. Small chapels like this lined the royal highway, El Camino Real, that was routed inland at this place to avoid the cliffs of the Rincon by the sea. The natives moved in around the adobe chapel, forming a town of small huts, Casitas, in Spanish, small casas or houses.   This is where Casitas Springs gets it's name. It's only a few miles south of Oak View and linked to the whole phenomena. Most who drive from Ventura to Ojai know the place by its power lines that knock out radio transmissions as one passes though the village. The power lines should have been a dead give away. Time travel, so they say, needs massive amounts of electrical energy.

Ghosts or rips in Time?

Then there were the ghost sightings and legends in Oak View. I should have known this was a strange place by the number of sightings from haunted houses to random apparitions of things that shouldn't be there.   Some believe that ghosts are spirits of the dead doomed to wander as earthbound souls. I have found that many do not seem to fill his definition. Many ghosts are more like rips in the fabric of time. Images of things that are out of place. Such as the lady who was crossing the river at Foster Park (near Casitas Springs) and was shocked to see a Spanish Conquistador in full armor standing by the bridge. The sighting is unique in many ways. Two people over a space of three years saw the same apparition. The armor they described was that of the early conquest of Mexico and nothing like the uniforms worn by the Spanish explorers who came with Father Serra in 1769. Their dress was more like the costumes worn in the American Revolution on the east coast. What had the two women seen? There are accounts of several early Spanish expeditions who traveled north seeking golden cities to plunder and vanished to history. Could this single soldier be from one such party?   Is this a ghost or simply a vision from the past?

Another ghost seen on a bridge is from a more recent time. He wears a derby hat and stands next to the Bridge over San Antonio Creek, just north of Casitas Springs. He is said to be the unhappy spirit of a doctor who was washed into the swollen creek in a storm. But, might he be a time slip as well? Following along the creek is a twisting two lane road that is rumored to have so many ghosts its sometimes called 'The Ghost Road." Here phantom riders gallop on spectral houses, ghosts with heads, vie with ghosts without them. A headless motorcyclist roars down creek road as the ghostly Lopez Lights dance in the creek bed. Why does this section of road have so many stories of haunts? Remarkably, there are also stories of UFOs on the same roadway. One woman saw a glowing basketball size light silently dash into the sky. Others saw a classic disk here in the late 1940's and more than a few whisper they have suffered abduction in the space. Then there are stories of strange creatures here. People have observed a huge glowing bat on Creek Road late at night as well as a thing in the creek bed. Many of the sightings focus on Camp Comfort a place where people go to find peace. The Bridge at Camp Comfort holds many stories from a cold spot to tales of ghostly children. The camp was once a sacred place to the Chumash Native People and legends say it was there that they held there terrible poison rituals. Spanish accounts say that the tribe would gather and each member would eat an acorn cookie. One of the cookies was filled with a deadly poison that would kill them. It was a sort of awful lottery of death and stories of sobbing ghosts and Native chants are linked to a stand of trees in the park. The Spanish Padres put a stop to this practice, seeing it as another sign of Satan's work.

Legends tell of a supernatural black dog on Creek Road. The beast was a Spanish Hound used to track down and intimidate natives. A Shaman refused to join the mission so a Spanish officer set the massive dog on the old man. Before he died, the Shaman put a curse on the Spanish. When he died under the jaws of the beast the spirit of the shaman left his body and went into the dog. It turned on its cruel master and ripped out his throat! The great black dog is also said to haunt the road way. That is the legend.

Why do so many things seem to happen on this Oak View lane? Could there be something in the place that causes things like this to be seen? I believe there is. It seems that some places on planet earth have a magnetic resonance that causes the past and present to converge from time to time. Such vortexes have been theorized for decades.

Time Vortex.

It is perhaps one of the most talked about story in the Twentieth Century. I feel it has been mislabeled as a ghost story when it is most likely a slip in time. It involved two English School Teachers, Miss Eleanor Jourdain and Miss Charlotte Moberley, on holiday in France. They visited the great Palace at Versailles just outside of Paris on a hot August 10th in 1901. As they wandered with their ever-present Baedeker's Guidebooks they found themselves in an ornate garden. They walked though the place as they even encountered people dressed in 18th Century tri-corn hats and green smocks. They even spoke with some of them, getting directions to the small Petit Trianon building. The man who directed them was wearing a wide brimmed hat and cape, they described him as a swarthy man with a pock-marked face. The strange thing was, they never asked for directions in the first place. Later they found the garden was gone! It had been ripped away after the French Revolution of 1789! The two woman had somehow walked into the 18th Century and out again! The two women wrote down what they saw and felt in their time travels. The first thing they both reported in their strange journey was a bout of indigestion. Then, they saw some sort of haze that rendered the landscape flat and two dimensional, as if they were props of a stage. Then things seemed to became normal for a time. They suspected it was a just the rich French food they had for lunch. In 1901 refrigeration was almost unknown and spoilage of foods was to be expected and tolerated. A year later they returned to Versailles and on this occasion, at the Hameau section, they saw two men in capes lacing sticks into a two wheeled cart.

Every detail of the strange journey was checked out from the costumes to the placement of the paths and they seemed to confirm that the two women had indeed stepped back in time. They compiled their findings into a book in 1911. It was titled "An Adventure" and it sold out five printings. Detractors tied to debunk the story saying the two ladies must have been mistaken or that they had accidentally walked into a costume party of some sort. The women were sure that they had seen what they had seen. It was years later than the family of a former royal gardener found a plan of the garden in a Paris attic. The paths were just as they two school teachers had described. What makes the case even more interesting is the fact that over the years others have seen things at Versailles. The two teachers were not even the first. In 1870 visitors to the place encountered "ghosts" at the palace. In 1928 two other English tourists saw a guard at Versailles dressed in the uniform of per-revolutionary France. Then in 1949 other tourists saw the apparition of a well dressed 18th Century woman they identified as Queen Marie Antoinette. This time she was holding a parasol. In May of 1955 more figures from the past were seen at the Petit Trianon. Two men and a woman, all dressed in yellow, were described. Resent sightings tell of seeing a woman in a pink dress and large hat. She is thought to be the ghost of Queen Marie Antoinette. All of the figures so far encountered are dressed in the styles of King Louis XVI. The two English schoolteachers researched the palace and believe they stepped back to the day August 5, 1789 and the dark man they saw, who gave them directions, was the Creole confidante of the Queen, Comte de Vaudreuil who often visited Versailles. They believed they had stepped back in time one hundred and twelve years!

The great French palace isn't the only place were time slips have been reported.

Another spot rumored to have a time vortex is located in the United States at the historic battlefield of Gettysburg. Here in July of 1863 men of the north and south fought a three day bloodbath that would decide outcome of the Civil War. Many such vortex sites seem to be triggered by human acts of violence. Possibly the bloody trauma of the French Revolution stimulated the time slip at Versailles. The massive battle at Gettysburg might have caused a time vortex to form in the small Pennsylvania town. The number of sightings here have filled several books. Like the case at Versailles, they are for the most part linked to the civil war battle. A single Union Soldier walks the halls of the Cashtown Inn, a group of Union soldiers are seen at the Gettysburg College as well. At the rocky boulder's nick named "Devil's Den," a single Confederate Soldier dressed in a scruffy uniform of the Texas volunteers walks. Some have even photographed the Texan standing a top the position. History records that a unit of Texans did defend the place, dying at their positions when over run by the Yankees. The old battlefield has a number of phantom riders, marching men and even a headless ghost.

As one might expect when a time vortex is opened, other images leak through. President Dwight Eisenhower and his wife Mamie retired in Gettysburg in 1950. Now their home is a museum honoring the General, World War Two hero and President. Mamie died in the house in 1979 but they have seen her apparition at the home. The encounters were so shocking that two employees threatened to quit. Also, at Spangler's Spring, on the historic battlefield, a phantom woman has been seen. This lady took her own life in 1880 when her adulterous affair was about to be uncovered. Like the former first lady she has nothing to do with the 1863 battle. What if these often told tales were not stories of earthbound ghosts but, images out of time? There are other places on planet Earth where such things happen.

There is believed by some that an invisible grid of lines covers the world like a net. This network of lines, called Ley Lines, is linked to many supernatural events. The theory is that humans can feel this energy and upon the sites they build their important buildings, such as churches, palaces, shrines, and such.

Places where the Ley lines meet are called Nodes and are said to have great supernatural energy. What if such a Node was bombarded with trauma, such as a battle or bloody revolution? Could it be that the site could somehow open a time portal of some sort? Events both human and natural might be enough to start the process of building a vortex.

Enter the Mullet Man

It all started with a simple ad placed in a local newspaper. Many thought it was a joke or some sort or a hoax. It read as follows:

> **"Wanted: somebody to go back in time with me. This is no joke.**
> **PO Box --- Oak View CA 93022. You'll get paid after we get Back. Must bring your own weapons. Safety not guaranteed. I have only done this once before."**

The bizarre ad attracted a great deal of interest and talk. Could a time traveler rally live in the town of Oak View, a community of 5,000. The ad even appeared on the popular Jay Leno TV show where it was the focus of laughter. The blogs took up the challenge on the net and the story of the Oak View time traveler was given a new life. The ad appeared in the net accompanied by a picture of a thick jawed man with a mullet hair do. The blog also featured the song "Push it to the limit" from the sound track of the movie "Scarface."

Many on the internet took up the challenge and tried to discover the name of the mysterious figure called "Mullet Man." One person managed to get a phone number and called it asking for the time traveler. The woman who answered listened then abruptly said "never call here again" and hung up. Another would be investigator got another phone number and this time got a recorded message that cryptically said: "Leave a message for Mark, Debbie, or Moses or Caesar." Are Moses and Caesar their children or perhaps their pets?

Some came to believe they might be the real Moses and Julies Caesar from history visiting Oak View from the past!

Then on the net came a new posting. A black and white picture of a Soldier from the Civil War. The soldier is holding a long rifle and has all the stilted pose of the 1860s. The man is wearing a mullet hair style and looks like the picture of Mullet Man! Is this proof that the time traveler made another journey back in time to the Civil War? This might explain the need to bring weapons. The old photograph is said to have been found in an attic. If it is an elaborate hoax perhaps the man behind it is a Civil War re-enactor and had the picture taken at a battle-reenactment. Several Civil War enthusiasts live in Oak View. Some now call the mysterious traveler "Mark" after the phone call but most still referred to him as the mullet man. The uniform is also indistinct. The cap and breaches appear to be Union, but the shirt Confederate. The rifle appears to be a Springfield mussel loader from the War Between the States

On a post titled "I found the Mullet Man" an investigator came to Oak View and looked up an address he had secured. He discovered the address was a vacant lot. Interestingly enough, at the site, he found a piece of paper on a fence from a "John Titor" a rumored time traveler made popular years ago by Art Bell. He claimed to be from the year 2036. Could the two be somehow linked?

John Titor—Time Traveler

In 2000 a fellow called in the Art Bell show claiming to be a time traveler. He would later give his name as John Titor and post answers on the web. For four months the fellow told of the future and gave dire predictions. He was always ready to give an answer to almost every question and he never sought out ways to capitalize on his fame. In four months he gave many responses, some redundant. Then, he was mysteriously gone. It was believed he returned to his home in central Florida in the year 2036.

John Titor's comments have spawned a number of web sites and there is even talk of a movie about the man and his journey though time. He was given to long-winded answers to questions from people on the net that were both compelling and enigmatic . He claimed that most of the world's population would die from Mad Cow disease, that terrible sickness he said, lies dormant within the body for years before it bursts out and kills the host. Among other things he told of a new American Civil War that would break out in 2005. The awful Civil War would pit urban populations against rural folks. This would be followed by a terrible World War that would pit Russia against The US and China. The Third World War would be fought with nuclear weapons, rendering much of the US poisoned and our present cities, ruble. The new capital would be built in Omaha. The present states would be condensed into five political bodies. By 2036 things had changed for the better and much of the destruction from the war would be cleaned up but the US would be a vastly different place. John Titor described an eco friendly future world where people produced their own food and power. Barter replaced much of the economic structure but, paper money was still in use and he told of getting a "paycheck." His vision of the future was a bit like a Hippie Commune with friends and family: The Waltons meet the Jetsons. His messages have been examined with some hints of future events seemingly coming to pass, such as the control of the federal government with the Patriot Act and the creation of non-lethal weapons. Still, major errors exist. There was no Civil War in 2005. He said that the most compelling year would be 2008 so we will need to wait on these dire predictions. Could Mr. Titor be from a parallel time line where the things he described happened, or was he a left over hippie with an over active imagination and a computer? Some denounced him as a hoax but others found worthy comments in his vision of the future. He denounced present people for their waist and greed and told our citizens to guard well our Constitutional rights—good advice for all to follow in a post 9-11 world. Titor never spoke of Global Warming or violent climate change. In 2036, so it seems, the seas hadn't flooded out Florida.

He claimed to be a soldier, part of an elite unit of five time travelers, set out on secret missions to retrieve things from the past. In this case it wasn't some artifact of America's Past but an old style IBM computer. One would think that over-aged computers would be of little value to the future. Far better I should think would be to go back in time to retrieve great works of literature or the papers of Abraham Lincoln. The style of conversation wasn't the discipline speech of a soldier, but of someone just chatting. Why would he be so forthcoming on the net? Wouldn't he fear that his comments might change the past and his own future?

His future wasn't all that great so maybe his mission was to change things? Why did he hang around in a world he held in contempt for four months, eating organic vegetables and only confiding his comments to the followers of Art Bell? Was it that he had to return in a preset window of some sort? One interesting comment that seems a bit far fetched. He said their wasn't any music in the future—nothing contemporaneous—they listened to music downloads from the past. So the future will be dominated by old Beach Boys and Beatles music?

His long list of comments do give us some insights on the future—at least to those who believe the stories of John Titor. But, then why was a note from John found at the location of Mullet Man? What is the link and is there a link at all?

Oak View, a unique place.

It is easy to dismiss the advertisement of a time traveler, a chrononaught if you will, as a hoax of some sort. Most did just that, thinking it was the product of one too many episodes of Star Trek. But, then, I live in Oak View and upon reading about the mysterious Mullet Man I had to reluctantly admit that strange things do happen in Oak View. The people who call this place home are an independent lot. Many times encounters with people on horseback take place. Are they just horse enthusiasts or are they Nineteenth Century cowboys somehow slipped into our own time? Then, there are the power failures. Never have I lived in a place where the lights go out so often. We see the power flicker and grab for our flashlights! Old style oil lamps decorate our mantel, not as nostalgic mementos of simpler times but working units that are put to good use when there is a blackout. These blackouts also come with massive power surges that can burn out and destroy electrical units. Only our surge protector saved our computer from being fried in the first surge (the power was out for two days). Sometimes strange sounds are heard and the sky lights up with bright flashes of light. Nicola Tesla isn't a resident but I could almost imagine he was conducting experiments just down the block.

The Search for Mullet Man

My search began when I wanted to find some answers to the riddle of mullet man. If it's a hoax, then let me in on the gag. If its not, then as a historian, I want to use this discovery to answer some of the great riddles of American History. From all I have read, there is nothing in quantum physics that states that time travel is impossible. The only rub seems to be our technology isn't advanced enough in the dawn of the Twenty-first Century. Perhaps the mullet man has come up with a new way to cross the time stream?

 To fill in the gaps I had to find mullet man. Living in Oak View gave me an advantage, or so I thought. Walking around the small town I saw no one who looked like the pictures, with or without the distinct hair style. I went to the local café again and again where everyone has breakfast and found no one like him. I went to the stores and didn't see him, even the barbershop was a failure. Perhaps the fellow was making it hard to find him on purpose or, maybe, he was on a time trip of some sort.

I used a page from his playbook and posted an article on the YourHub.com section of the Ventura County Star Newspaper. I asked if the Mullet Man would contact me or if anyone who knew him would come forward. I would keep his identity secret if I could just interview the time traveler.   Next, I made posters seeking information and put them on the local bulletin boards in hope of stimulating a response from the Time traveler or Hoaxer, which ever he was.   I waited in vain to get any answers.

I had to ask myself where in time I would go, if I had the chance. One location came to mind almost instantly: a grassy knoll in Dallas, Texas, on the November afternoon of the 23rd in 1963. Then I could see who or what was there as President Kennedy drove across the plaza. Another destination would be a bedroom in a house August 4th of 1903 in Fall River, Massachusetts where a Miss Lizzie Borden lived. What really happened that bloody day? Maybe I would attempt to change history and go to a theater box in Washington DC on April 14th of 1865, where President Lincoln was watching a comedy. Maybe, if someone had blocked the door to the box…. I let my mind reel, hoping against all hope, that Oak View somehow held the key to time travel.   Only the mysterious Mullet Man whoever he is, would have the answers for me.   If I have learned anything in my years of ghost hunting it is that patience does pay off in the end.

The Call.

It was 9:30 when the call came. I picked up the phone thinking it was a friend or relative on the other end. Who else would call at this hour? It was too late for the telemarketers with there bothersome spiels.   There was silence on the line at first.
I will present to you the conversation as best I recall, I wasn't ready to hear from Mullet Man. He wouldn't catch me unaware again.

(Voice) Are you Richard Senate?

(Richard) Yes? Who are you and how can I help you? (I thought it must be someone with a ghost problem as I get calls like that all the time.)

(Voice) You're the guy looking for the Mullet Man?

(Richard) Yes, do you know anything about him?

(Voice) You might say that.

(Richard) Do you know his name? Does he live in Oak View?

(Voice) Yes, he lives here. I know his name too.

(Richard) It's all a hoax, right? The time travel and all that, no one can....

(Voice) It's real. He's done it and he's doing it now.

(Richard) Are you certain? Are you sure he's not just giving you a line of guff?

(Voice) It's no joke.   I wanted to let you know that it's not a game. He's real.

(Richard) (by now I was quickly taking notes) I want to know more. Where is his time machine?

(Voice) (Laughing now softly) There really isn't one—you don't drive back in time in a sort of VW, its more like a door you open. I've said too much. Good night.

(Richard) Wait, I have a question for you. (The voice was replaced by a dial tone).

It was over in less than two minutes but it left me clutching the phone receiver as my heart raced in my chest. I had the thing still at my ear listening to the sound of the dial tone as I tried to make sense of it all. In the flyers and articles I had distributed I never once put down my phone number. How had he gotten my private phone number?

I didn't recognize the voice. It was male, I was sure about that, there wasn't any trace of accent nor anything noticeable in the background. The connection was clear so I could well imagine it was placed from somewhere within the township of Oak View.

I put down the phone and did what my years of ghost hunting trained me to do—I wrote everything down while it was still fresh in my mind.   I had jotted down a few notes about the time traveling VW and I put them into the narration I have presented to you.

He implied he had said too much. It seemed that he didn't trust me. Who was he afraid of and why? Were there people trying to steal his invention or were there some dark forces out there attempting to learn his identity?   Clearly, I would need to earn his trust if he should ever call again.   He wanted to make sure I knew Mullet Man wasn't a joke. He risked everything to make sure I was told it wasn't a prank.

I had to admit that it could well have been a jokester after all. My phone number is in the book and I am not that hard to find. I resolved to keep the whole thing a secret and wait just to see if he would call again. This time I would be ready with a pad of paper and a pen at the phone.   The week that followed was a tense one as I jumped when ever the phone rang. Everything seemed to take on a sinister feel. Strange sounds woke me in the night, the sounds as if someone loudly dragging something in the street at four a.m. There were gun shots in the night as well. Once, there was a scream and moan in the night. Just local kids making noise and setting off fireworks or was it all something else? I would not be forced to wait long.

The Second Call

It was a hot Saturday when the next call came. My wife and daughter had left to go to the nursery to purchase some plants for the garden.

I was resting when the phone rang. I answered it glancing at the pad of paper on the nightstand. I said "Hello," then the familiar voice answered.

(Voice) This is Richard?

(Richard) Yes. (I was scrambling for the pad and pen now).

(Voice) I called before. You said you had questions, I had to hang up then.

(Richard) I have about a million questions to ask you.

(Voice) Yes?

(Richard) What's your name?

(Voice) If I told you it might place you in danger, you and your family.

(Richard) Are you the Mullet Man?

(Voice) That's what you say.

(Richard) Danger from whom?

(Voice) Better to say from what.

(Richard) Do you travel in time?

(Voice) (there was a long pause) Yes.

(Richard) How many times now?

(Voice) Now? Five times so far. Two times to the Civil War.

(Richard) The Civil War?

(Voice) 1862 and 1864. I will never go back to that time again. It was the most nightmarish thing imaginable. People blown to bits, guts flying, arms and legs everywhere. The smells made me sick both times. It was nothing like the movies I can tell you that.

(Richard) Were you with the North or the South?

(Voice) Once I was with the Union and another time I served with the Rebels. They were the bravest men I have ever seen. They just stood up and let the shells rip them to pieces. They never flinched but just took it. It wasn't a war really, it was mass murder. I found the Rebels were much more friendly and open.

(Richard) What unit were you with? What battles?

(Voice) Sharpsburg and Cold Harbor, I think. Things were very confusing for infantrymen. Half the time you didn't know what you were doing, all you were sure of was that people were shooting at you.

(Richard) Did you see any famous men like General Mead or (Robert E.) Lee?

(Voice) I didn't call to talk about the war. I called to warn you.

(Richard) Warn me? Am I in danger?

(Voice) I think so. I found you, others can as well.

(Richard) What others? Other time travelers?

(Voice) No, people from the government. The NSA wants me and will use every effort to stop my research and take my invention. In the wrong hands….. I can't say more.

(Richard) What sort of danger?

(Voice) (Whispering) They come in pairs. They will have any excuse to try and get into your house. Don't let them in. Don't volunteer anything to them or to anyone who calls you. Even if it's President Bush himself don't tell him a thing. Your phone isn't tapped yet, I can tell from here, but expect that it might be at some future time.

(Richard) Are you sure this isn't an unwarranted fear on your part?

(Voice) It's real. Don't believe all you hear on the news. What ever you do don't break any laws. Don't speed or lie on your taxes because that will give them an opportunity to get to you.
(Richard) I don't speed. I think your being paranoid.

(Voice) Believe what you will, but remember my words. Good day.

The phone went dead in my hand. Was this some nut I was talking with spinning all sorts of conspiracy theories or should I beware ? I went over the notes I had made as we were speaking, cleaning up my short hand and trying to remember what the voice had said. My phones might be tapped? Pairs of men would be coming to the house. I half expected men in black to appear with sunglasses and business suites. Such people would stick out in a place like Oak View.

Later that afternoon I heard the doorbell and when I opened the door two young men in white shirts and black ties were standing grim faced on my threshold. They had pocket protectors. They were Mormon Missionaries. Interestingly, they looked a bit old to be missionaries and they both wore dark glasses.

They gave their names as Elder this and Elder that, from Utah and asked if we had read the Book of Mormon. They wanted to come inside. An alarm bell when off in my head.
I told them "no" but they were persistent about wanting to come in. One then said he wanted to use the bathroom. They spoke in a sort of monotone very unlike the Mormons I had encountered before. I said no firmly but they still tried to open the screen door. I slammed the main door closed and locked it. They stood for a long time, then walked away. As I watched them walk down the street though the peep hole I was shaking all over. I keep telling myself they were

just Missionaries, that's all, just two young men seeking converts. I tried to tell myself I was just getting paranoid. I looked again down the road and they had vanished away completely. Was I becoming as crazy as my mysterious caller?

Then came the mystery phone calls.

They called at random times and when you answered the call there was only dead air on the line. It was like someone just wasn't speaking. The calls came in the mornings as well as the evenings. Were they telemarketers who had made some mistake in dialing or was there something more mysterious? I began to imagine all sorts of things. Maybe the house was being bombarded by microwaves in an attempt to listen in on what we were talking about. Sometime I imagined that things seemed to have been moved when I got home from work. Had someone broken into the house? Were they planting "bugs" in our home? I began to think that people were watching the house as I left. I recall that once a black van with tinted windows followed my car all the way to Ventura. The thing tailgated me until I got to Main Street, Ventura, then peeled away. Was it just some young van nut or something sinister? I began to put simple booby traps in the house, a bit of paper in the doorjam. A line of thread on the threshold in hope of seeing if my delusions were true. I came home once and saw the thread was broken! A chill raced down my spine. The door was unlocked but, I discovered my daughter had simply came home early. A week later I came home to another shocker. There was a note on the door hooked to the nail where Christmas Wreaths were hung during the holidays.
It said simply, "The House is Clean—No bugs—MM" The words were in some wide tipped felt pen. That's all it said. How had the man managed to enter the house? For some reason I expected a phone call that night. Maybe it was a hunch or just logic. Why would he sweep the house if he wasn't going to call me? I felt that my relationship with the Mullet Man was about to enter a new phase.

Was all this just some sort joke? Maybe I was being set up for some elaborate scam? Someone would call and ask for money to fix his time machine –his "flux capacitor" needed fixing and for a mere $2,000 I too could go back in time. Then after getting the money he would vanish. I have been around the block a few time and felt I could spot any scammer.

The Third Call

It came at 9:45 that night. I caught it on the kitchen phone. My pen and paper were ready and I took notes.

(Richard) Hello?

(Voice) Did you get my note?

(Richard) Is this MM?

(Voice) (chuckling sound) Yes. You need a new computer too. Yours should be in a museum. That password "Ghostlamp" It took me four minutes to hack into your system.

(Richard) I will change my password tonight. Do you often break into people's homes?

(Voice) Only people I care about.

(Richard) You said there were no bugs?

(Voice) Yes, but you are under observation.

(Richard) By whom?

(Voice) Division "Y" of the NSA. They deal with time travel. They have been here for over a year now trying to find me.

(Richard) Can we meet face to face?

(Voice) (Long pause) Yes. In time we will.

(Richard) Why did you call tonight?

(Voice) I would have called sooner but I had to check you out first. You might have been an agent of the NSA. I can't afford to take chances.

(Richard) Did you check me out?

(Voice) Yes, having a time machine helps. Do you recall the man selling magazines in 1969? I came to your white house on the corner of Dalton and Lexington in Ventura. It was about two in the afternoon, May 18th? We spoke for some time. Do you remember the pushy customer you had at your job at Thrifty Drug Store in 1973? I visited you in 1994 as well. You give great tours I might add. They were all me. I did a bit of snooping as well just to see if you are who you say you are.

(Richard) I'm to be impressed with this? You could have gotten that information in public records. I do have a vague memory of a pushy college student trying to sell me magazines but, I guess everyone has a memory like that.

(Voice) Perhaps.

(Richard) Well, now that I am "checked out" why have you called me?

(Voice) I need help, I need your help

(I began to think this was where he would set me up for a con job. His next request would be for money. I felt sure about it so I decided to meet the challenge head on.)

(Richard) I want to let you know I don't have any money.

(Voice) Yes, I know the size of your bank account and your income. This isn't about money. I need you to do something for me.

(Richard) Is it illegal? I will have nothing to do with drugs….

(Voice) Nothing like that.

(Richard) Tell me about the future. What's going to happen. You have traveled to the future haven't you?

(Voice) Yes, three times I have traveled to the future, so far. What do you want to know?

(Richard) Everything. What was the first time you did it?

(Voice) It was simple. I stepped into the vortex and I was there. It did make me dizzy, it always does. It took just a few seconds and it does tingle like an electric shock. It took me a little time to adjust.

(Richard) Where did you go?
(Voice) Santa Barbara, (California) State Street.

(Richard) Why There? Why not New York or Paris?

(Voice) I wanted someplace I knew.

(Richard) How far into the future did you go?

(Voice) 2033—March 12th if you must know the exact date. I can't get the day exact, at least not yet, I am good with the year and month. It was raining at the time. I came out on the corner of State and Ortega.

(Richard) What was it like? Were their flying cars?

(Voice) (Laughter) No. There were few cars on the road. They were more like boxes in shape and they were silent.

(Richard) Were they electric?

(Voice) No—at least I don't think so. They may have been natural gas. Why do people always ask about cars?

(Richard) What else did you see?

(Voice) It was not that much different, but there were more awnings over the street –bright striped ones. There were large screens on the street and cameras everywhere.
There were lots people walking the streets and policemen in pairs. They had helmets on and body armor.

(Richard) Like the storm troopers in Star Wars?

(Voice) No, more like riot police today. The uniforms were light blue. They looked at me but they didn't see me as a threat and they just let me pass. I was looking for a newspaper.

(Richard) Did you find one?

(Voice) They don't have newspapers in the future. I didn't see anything like a newspaper, not even a magazine. I went into something that looked like a drug store and to go in you had to pass a sort of archway of electronic sensors. They didn't go off so I went in. There were rows of glass fronted cabinets with all sorts of bottles and colorful labels like "sunshine" and "ruby breeze." I didn't know what they were but they were expensive. A single bottle, the size of an aspirin bottle, was one hundred and seventy-five dollars. There was a large screen TV on the wall, maybe five by eight feet. From it I got the date. It was playing a news show. Two people were watching and two more shopping. They were wearing plastic ponchos and close fitting hats.
(Richard) What was on the News?

(Voice) They were talking about a war in North Africa. It took me a while to figure out that we, America, was involved. America was now called The North American Union or NAU. I saw a map and we had a lot more states—Mexico and Canada and Cuba were all one nation. The flag had the same stripes but an eagle in the field with leaves around it.

(Richard) What else did it say?

(Voice) The Allies, The UEC and US, had won a great victory over General Vallee and the South African Union. They had a video of the general who was a dressed like black Napoleon. It had pictures of his troops running away and thousands captured. They flashed a picture of the globe and the South Africans seem to own most of the continent.

(Richard) Was it like a propaganda piece.

(Voice) Yeah, there was music, like John Philip Sousa and lots of flags. There was a shot of the President. A man with a beard and long hair. Looked a bit like Shakespeare. The name was Branigan Bolwers I think. He wasn't wearing a tie but a sort of scarf with a jewel in the center.

(Richard) Was he saying anything?

(Voice) He was saying something about the heroic actions of the Big Red one in the battle but I didn't get a chance to hear more.

(Richard) Why is that?

(Voice) A clerk dressed a bit like a doctor asked if he could assist me I my selection.

(Richard) What did you say to him?

(Voice) I didn't want to look too out of place so I smiled and said "no."

(Richard) What did you do next.

(Voice) He said "Just getting out from the rain?" I nodded and he said "sound" That's all.
Well I left after that and went down towards the Art Museum. The thing was still there but it now had a glass dome on top of the building. The street had lots of restaurants, or at least I guessed they were Restaurants, people were eating things that looked like

oversized 'Hot Pockets' and drinking from odd tankards. Like German beer steins?

(Richard) Why didn't you go in and try something?

(Voice) I didn't have any of the money they used. I didn't want to invite attention. My clothes did seem a bit off. There was a guard station in front of the Art Museum. So I didn't get too close. There was a statue in front of the place, maybe ten feet tall. There was a sign. It was Saint Barbara. I saw a woman following me. You get the nack for telling when your being followed. I could feel it on the back of my neck. I kept going til I got to a theater. It was the Grenada I believe but greatly re-done. They had a moving sign that read " Dr. Kildares wondrous Holiday." I don't know if it was a play or a movie or something else. Little clips showed a handsome blond guy with a sailor cap with a woman wearing shorts and sick-on things on her nipples.

(Richard) Like a swim suit?

(Voice) I think so. I didn't get to look because I was walking away from the woman with big sunglasses. She had a green hat pulled low and a layer of clothing. I turned down an ally to see if she was really following me. I ducked into a doorway as she started to talk into what looked like a wrist watch.

(Richard) What did you do then?

(Voice) I pulled the plug. I got out as quick as I could. I Stepped into the doorway and back to the present. I remember I was dizzy for four hours.

(Richard) What doorway?

(Voice) Its part of the time traveler—I can open it to come back any place—To go back or forward is harder and I need a large source of energy. You will see in due time.

(Richard) I will see you time machine?

(Voice) Only if you are nice. I must go now. I picked up an intruder.

(Richard) What sort of intruder?

(Voice) Helicopter. Good night my friend.

The phone went dead as he hung up. I listened and hear the faint sound of a helicopter far above Oak View, I wrote down as much as I could. I jotted down what I could recall of the NAU and the War in Africa the President who looked like Shakespeare and the lack of newspapers. The world seemed a suspicious place more like Nazi Germany than America. The future sadly wasn't a happy utopia but a sort of police state. I had a hard time sleeping afterwards. I didn't hear from my mysterious friend for ten days. The name of the new nation haunted me. The North American Union. It was a day later that it hit me that I had heard of it on an old episode of the British Science Fiction TV show "Dr Who." In this show America was called the North American Union in the future. I wondered in my contact was a fan of British Science Fiction?

The Forth Call

The call came just as I sat down to dinner. I assumed it was some aggressive Telimarketer of some sort and was about to tell him to buzz off when I heard his familiar voice.

(Voice) I caught you at a bad time. I will call back in 20 minutes. He then hung up.

I rushed though my dinner so I would be ready for the call. I should have taken my time because it came two hours later. I had almost thought he had forgotten his promises to call back. I jumped when the phone rang.

(Voice) Richard, Are you still awake?

(Richard) Yes, Are you Ok? We really need to meet. I want to see what you look like.

(Voice) All in due time. Are you still interested in the future?

(Richard) Yes.

(Voice) I just came back from a new trip. This time I managed to get some money by hocking some things at a pawn shop, or I should say a future Redemption/ Antique Center. I was back maybe a full day this time and I took notes. You should feel proud, I went back for you.

(Richard) Back to Santa Barbara?

(Voice) Nope, this time I tried to go back to LA. But….

(Richard) But What?

(Voice) there isn't any in the future. It's gone. Only a basted wasteland with a few twisted steel ruins and part of the City Hall left.

(Richard) What happened? Earthquake? The big one?

(Voice) War, the city was basted by an atom bomb. Four million people died—they think.

(Richard) Who, who did it? Terrorists?

(Voice) Chinese. There was a war. Pearl Harbor, San Diego were also hit. China lost more, maybe 100.000 million were nuked before we put a stop to it all. The war only lasted a month and a half, the nuclear part only five days. People will be suffering the after effects for fifty years.

(Richard) Where did you go?

(Voice) Santa Monica. It was spared from the blast. They still have libraries and I spent about three hours at one off Ocean Avenue. Did you know they expanded the pier? It's like a Disneyland then. It has all sorts of rides and restaurants and dance halls built in almost every style, excepting Chinese.

(Richard) What else did you find?

(Voice) Let me get my notes out for you. Not a lot of paper in the future. The North American Union was started when Western Canada Joined with the United States in 2019, Eastern Canada joined in 20, and Cuba in 21, Mexico Joined after the second revolution in 2017 becoming part in 2022, The capital is now in Bolder, Colorado after Washington was lost in 2019.

(Richard) the Chinese blew it up?

(Voice) No—This was terrorism from Arabia this time. They flew a private jet with a small nuke into the White House.

(Richard) Like 9-11?

(Voice) Worse. The Government was ripped up. The secretary of state was in London at the time came back until elections could be held. Everyone else was killed or sick. It was a specially designed dirty bomb. Two, to three million died. It killed people all the way into Baltimore. The Navy launched rockets almost at once. Arabia was hit hard. No one complained.

(Richard) When did this happen?

(Voice) August of 2019.

(Richard) What else did you find?

(Voice) They use nuclear power now and they have it so that they don't have any waste products. They are even reusing old spent rods for power. They have power stations up and down the coast in big silo shaped plants.

(Richard) What about earthquakes?

(Voice) They have that solved. People use a lot more power but there are fewer people. Maybe half of what we have today. Lots of empty buildings and whole housing tracts are abandoned.

(Richard) Was it the war?

(Voice) Yes, the war took many lives but most people were lost to Ebola, they call it E-Boy Fervor in the future. In two years 72 million were lost—at least that's what the history books said. There were huge mausoleums set up for the dead. These things are maybe five stories high that look a bit like Ancient Greek Temples. No real count on how many died around the world but it may have been a billion or more. The library was mostly full of American information.

(Richard) Did you get a chance to walk around much?

(Voice) Yes, I found the pawn shop and went to a restaurant. You order at your table with a small computer. They don't have waiters, at least not in the places I visited. The prices were in dollars but just outrageous. I had a California Burger and turnip fries for $78 and a weak shake in a small glass that had almost no taste. One good thing, no tipping in the future.

(Richard) Turnip Fries?

(Voice) No potatoes on the menus. But the turnips were spiced and were OK.   Lots of the stuff were dishes from Eastern Europe and the Middle East. Borsches was there, what the Hell is Borsches?

(Richard) I think it's a Russian Soup?

(Voice) There were air raid shelters well marked on the streets. One was on Third Street and Santa Monica.   Some people were wearing surgical masks of some sort as well. I didn't see a lot of children on the street but it was a weekday and they may have been in school or something. Lots of posters were up now showing people of different races and cultures working together. There were warning of watching for SA. Subversive Activities I found out.   The war had traumatized people. Lots of people were walking around like zombies.

(Richard) Who was in charge in this future America?

(Voice) I got to go. I will get back with you soon.

(Richard) When can we meet?

At that the phone line went dead once again. I pondered what Turnip fries would taste like and how America had blundered into yet another terrible war, this one that saw the end of whole cities. It seemed the world was still a dangerous place in the future. I began to wonder if the voice of the time traveler was pulling my leg. Was he just giving me enough information to keep me interested or was this the real thing? My questions about the man would continue. I needed to meet with him face to face. A week would pass before he called again. This time it came in the morning.

The Fifth Call

It was in the morning when it came. My wife had left early and I half expected it was a friend of mine with information on a ghost book I was working on. I recognized the voice at once.

(Voice) I hope I didn't wake you?

(Richard) No, I was about to get up anyway.

(Voice) I am sorry I had to go so abruptly. I was being followed and my line tapped into.

(Richard) Who was doing this?

(Voice) The NSA or the CIA. I am not sure now.

(Richard) We need to meet face to face. I need to see whom I am talking with.

(Voice) I don't know if its safe just now.

(Richard) Is the phone being tapped right now?

(Voice) No, its safe.

(Richard) I insist we meet.

(Voice) Where should we meet? It's got to be a public place. I will insist on that.

(Richard) How about the Highway 33 coffee shop?

(Voice) I go there a lot. No, I believe the forces that wish to capture me know I like that spot.

(Richard) Then you pick a place.

(Voice) What about the breakfast place M and J's Café on the Main Street.

(Richard) It's just across the street from the Highway 33 coffee shop. Why would it be safer?

(Voice) It just is. We shall meet next Thursday at 8:30 a.m.

(Richard) How will I know you? Will you be wearing a gardenia on your lapel?

(Voice) You will not know me. You see, I know you. I will be disguised as well. You can buy me breakfast. They have a good hash and eggs breakfast. Don't be late. Remember 8:30.

At that he hung up once again.

I began to wonder about my contact. What was his plan and why was he so secretive. Was it all some elaborate plan to scam money out of me? At present it looked like all I would get stuck with was the bill for breakfast.

THE MEETING?

I was able to walk down to the café from my house. It was foggy and cool as it is many mornings at Oak View. I was looking to see if there was someone watching. I scanned every car and bus for anyone wearing a Mullet hairdo. The people were a normal group for Oak View. There was a bearded old timer who looked like Gabby Hays the cowboy star, a women who could have been an over aged movie star with too much make up and a tattoo on her ankle, a burley man who could have been a biker gang leader or a tattoo artist but no one who resembled the image of Mullet Man with or without his distinct hairstyle.

I got to the quaint restaurant at 8:20 and took a booth as the waitress got me a cup of coffee. She knew my likes and got me the drink without waiting to ask. When she returned she inquired about Debbie, my wife, and I told her that she was at work at this time and I was expecting a friend. She nodded and left.

I sipped the coffee. It was rich and strong the way I like it. M & J Café had great food and better coffee. My wife and I are regulars here and I guess we are well known by the staff and owner. I kept my eye on the door not really knowing what to expect. I thought about my strange friend and his talk of time travel. As a historian I should have asked more questions on the trips he made to the past. I am a fan of the Civil War. If he was pulling my leg I could have detected it better if he gave me data on the past. This stuff on the future is anyone's guess. I can't research the future. Some of the things he told me seemed beyond belief. It seemed that when ever I asked a detailed question he would sign off. Was that because he hadn't thought of a cool answer or what?

I glanced at my watch and saw that it was 8:35. I craned my neck and looked out the window in hopes of seeing my "friend" walking towards the café. There was nothing there. The waitress came and asked if I would like to order. I told her I was waiting for a friend but to check back in a few minutes.

My heart was racing in my chest now. I felt he would step in at any time with some ridiculous costume or disguise. The door opened. It was a fat man and his wife. I didn't see anyone else. They walked past me without a glance and took a booth deeper in the restaurant.

My watch now read 8:45. I jotted down the time in a note book I had slipped into my pocket before I left the house. The waitress came back with a smile to refill my coffee cup.

"Want to order?" She asked.

"Why not? I'll have the hash and eggs, over easy, sour dough toast and cottage fries. Just keep the coffee coming."

"Your friend coming?" she asked with a sad face.

"Who knows? Maybe he was delayed?"

"They say there was a big accident down at Casitas Springs," she said. "Maybe that delayed him.
 A truck hit an SUV and rolled it. They have police cars all over."

A sudden chill raced down my back. Had the forces that wanted to stop the time traveler managed to stop him permanently? Maybe it was just an accident, I thought. They have lots of accidents at that spot, I have seen half a dozen there in the last two years.

I glanced up and saw two men sitting in a small booth by the window looking at me. They had shifted themselves to do so. Both men were wearing dark glasses and tan shirts. One smiled at me, while the other slowly nodded his head.

Somehow I knew these were not my friends. A wave of panic surged up from the pit of my stomach. It was an acidic reaction that left the stinging taste of bile in my mouth. The two men turned and faced each other but, like me, they too were looking out the window. They looked like they were waiting for someone as well.

My food arrived but my appetite had left.

I played with my food and took the time to study the two men. They both were wearing work boots and their hair was cut in a short military style. One was sort of bull necked. One man had an expensive watch with a gold link band. It didn't look like the sort of watch a working man would wear. Maybe my mind was playing tricks on me. They could have been line men for the phone company or maybe oil workers.

I kept my eyes open for anyone coming into the café. More came but I felt this encounter wasn't going to happen—at least not today.

I managed to eat some of my food, finished the coffee and waited. People came and left all except me and the two tan clad men. I wanted to wait them out. They didn't leave only glancing at me and their watches. I checked it was 10:30 now and I decided to make a move. I took the bill and paid it but, rather than going, I sat back down and continued to sip my coffee and nibble on my bread.

The two men were eyeing me. The thought occurred to me that they might be my mysterious friend—or two of his confederates stationed here to play upon my fears of some wild government conspiracy. The Mullet Man may well be nothing but an elaborate scam. I was seized with the idea that maybe I should go to their table and ask about Mullet Man.   But, that would be too bold, they would deign everything. Besides that, their was every chance they were just a couple of guys having a late breakfast. If they were just guys they wouldn't do anything when I left. I got up and I noticed one of the men watching me. I saw a stack of bills on the table next to the meal ticket. They were ready to move. I went not to the door but to the bathroom in the back of the café.

I thought their might be a back way out of the place. I could hear the owner talking to his Latino cook.   I checked but I couldn't find any sign of a back door. When I looked up, the two men were gone and the waitress was cleaning the table. They had vanished.

Then a new thought hit me. Maybe they were waiting outside to grab me? I shook my head. Now I was getting as paranoid as my friend on the phone.

I left slowly, there was no one present. I kept an eye on the vehicles to see if my two large friends were in one of them. As far as I could see they were empty. I walked back to the Old Ojai Road behind the Restaurant in hopes I could see if I was being followed.

There was on one there. I cross over to the Oak View Market and dashed in hoping to see anyone there. I mindlessly looked at the meat. The clerk must have thought me insane. But, I was watching the door to see if anyone would come in. No one did. I left and crossed the street then took two street to get back to my house. Maybe the two men were just in the Café for a late breakfast, I thought, I was working myself into a tizzy over nothing. I walked up to my house and saw a white van parked on the street not far from my house. I know the cars on my street and this wasn't one of them. The men in the Van were wearing dark glasses. They were the same two men I had seen before. They didn't wait, they started the engine and pulled off. I was scared now. If the nameless voice wanted to scare me he was doing a good job. Maybe one of the men was the person on the phone. Or maybe they were just workmen who had nothing to do but chat in front of my house.

THE SIXTH CALL

The next call came three days later. It was early in the morning when the phone began to ring.

(Voice) Good Morning Richard. How are you feeling?

(Richard) Where were you. I waited for hours.

(Voice) You saw them didn't you. If I had come into the Café everyone would have been killed. The place would have been blown up and the explosion blamed on a "Gas Leak." You would be surprised at how many gas leaks are cover ups for the powers that be.

(Richard) I saw some strange men but how do I know you didn't send them?

(Voice) You believe that?

(Richard) I don't know what to believe. For all I know you were one of the men.

(Voice) (Laughter) Me? They almost got me with a truck at Casitas.

(Richard) I heard about that.

(Voice) they got some poor slob who had the misfortune to drive a van like mine. I have gotten rid of the van. I don't think they have traced my new car.

(Richard) How do you know they haven't bugged my phone or my house?

(Voice) They did. I cleaned your house of all bugs yesterday. They will be back but it will be a few days. I have some surprises in store for them.

(Richard) What do you mean? I will not condone violence in my ….

(Voice) Don't get your panties in a knot. Time travel has some advantages in getting back at people—I can step back a day or two and do things to their truck. I can make a few phone calls. Remember the Pizza that came a few days ago?

(Richard) The one that wasn't ordered? I thought it was a mistake.

(Voice) Pepperoni and Olives right? I thought you might like it. It was no mistake. It was a sort of demonstration to some of my friends.

(Richard) Now I am a lab rat for you? I want to tell your side of the story to the world. I want to let people know that your not a joke.

(Voice) I understand. I'm just having fun with you. I must tell you that I don't have much time left. They are getting closer. If they have too they will take out the whole of Oak View and blame it on something like a terrorist attack or accident.

(Richard) I find that hard to believe.

(Voice) Believe it.

(Richard) What are you going to do?

(Voice) Leave. Use my invention to escape in time. I have been thinking of a spot in the San Fernando Valley in the 1950s or the 1940s. Far enough back to escape, but not so far back as to not have a few connivances. Then there is also the future but, as you know, it doesn't look that great for America in the future. I still plan on more future trips soon. I will be a rich man in the past. I plan to invest in IBM Stocks and AT&T. All under an assumed name naturally. I may even give you a hand or maybe I already have and don't know it yet.

(Richard) This is all very confusing for me. Why couldn't the government track you?

(Voice) They don't have a time transport yet. That's why they want me. They want me alive so they can waterboard the secret out of me. They will never get it. Time travel is too important to be trusted to the government. Imagine President Bush with time transportation?

(Richard) Maybe he could have stopped what happened on nine-eleven?

(Voice) You are so trusting Richard. You will swallow any lie they put out.

(Richard) Are you saying that nine-eleven was a plot by the Government? I am sorry but I can't believe that. President Bush is a lot of things but he would never sit back and watch the murder of thousands of fellow Americans.

(Voice) You really believe he's in charge? You really think the powers that be would trust a bumpkin to run important things? There are forces at work here that you can't understand.

(Richard) You're sounding like some kind of conspiracy nut.

(Voice) Yeah, I am the time traveler and you are a ghost hunter. No one is going to believe anything you write. Maybe that's why the powers that be haven't stopped our conversations. They know they can paint you as a nut case even if you try to publish anything. I guess I am a fool to even trust you.

(Richard) You can trust me.

(Voice) Can I? How long would you hold out if they had your wife or kids? Not long I believe. You would spill your guts to them. Then they would make sure you   spend the rest of your days in a mental hospital in a drug induced daze. You would not be the first or the last. Your reputation will be ruined and you turned into a mental case. This is even if they let you live.   Your best chance is to ride the tiger through.

(Richard) What do you mean?

(Voice) Only publication will insure some safety for you. That or you can hitch a ride with me back where you can be safe. You will be safe back in the past. You like Ike don't you? You might even get a chance to see Dick Nixon before he becomes president.

(Richard) What about my wife and family? Can they go back?

(Voice) Nope, just one can accompany me. Without you they will be safe. They will watch over them to see if you come back for a visit. You will be a wanted man. You will have a price on your head worse than Osama Bin Laden. Once you go back, you can't return.

(Richard) I don't know.

(Voice) Think about it. You may not have a choice soon. I have to go now—something isn't right. See you in a few days…

At that, the phone when dead in my hand. He had hung up on me once again. I was a bit fearful now. What if it wasn't a joke or scam? What if I really was in danger? I thought back at the two men at the café. They looked like they could have been killers.   Three weeks passed before there was another call.
I was starting to get jumpy. Even my family started to notice that I was getting grumpy. I was hooked but I didn't want to be pulled into some sort of scam. So far no one had asked me for anything but I know enough about con men to know they can wait and work a mark waiting for a big payday. Still I caught myself looking out the windows and seeking men out with dark glasses. The days passed slowly and I jumped when the phone rang like a teenage girl waiting for a hot date.   Then it came.

The Seventh Call

It was maybe 10 pm when the phone rang. I picked it up quickly as my wife gave me a funny look. I suspected I was getting calls from some woman. I dare not tell her the full story of my mysterious caller.

(Richard) Hello?

(Voice) It's me. I just got back in town.

(Richard) where did you go?

(Voice) To a place I never thought I would visit again-- the Civil War. July of 1863 if your interested. To the site of a great battle.

(Richard) Gettysburg? My ancestor William Perry Senate fell there on July 2, 1863.

(Voice) Nope.

(Richard) Where then?

(Voice) Vicksburg on the Mississippi River. This time I was with General Grant's Troops. I was working with a Sutler, I wasn't a soldier this time. They were checking people out because they feared spies. I didn't want to get myself shot.

(Richard) Sutler? (I had heard the term)

(Voice) We sold things to the soldiers. Paper, tobacco, sweets, all sorts of little things. I even sold French Postcards of naked ladies. They were very popular. I could get a whole fifty cents for them. I took only coin—no shin plasters.

(Richard) Shin-whats ?

(Voice) Small paper bills for change—like 50 and 25 cents. Two bits and four bits, you know.

(Richard) Did you see the battle?

(Voice) sure enough did and it was something awful to behold. The sky was lit up with shells and bombs. There were rockets too. Gunboats in the River erupting like volcanoes onto the town. The Rebs fired back too. I was out of range but they gave as well as they got. For a time it looked as if the town was in flames.
The horror of the thing was unimaginable. Arms and legs flying this way and that, people a screamin' and calling out for their mothers. The hospital was more a butcher shop or torture chamber. Lots of men died while they were sawing off limbs. The smell is what I recall the most. It was a stink I shall never forget.

(Richard) Your talking funny. Why is that?

(Voice) I been back there and that's how they spoke. It's a habit, like an accent. It will wear away in time.

(Richard) how was it back there?

(Voice) Hot, really hot. The men were all talking about McClellan and his run for the presidency. Not a lot of people like Lincoln and many called him a buffoon and a monkey. Most liked Grant, even if a great many thought he was a drunk.

(Richard) What about the Confederates?

(Voice) Most thought they were misguided fools for following evil leaders. A handful saw the as abominations who deserved to be sent into hell. There wasn't much talk about slavery even when the men were drinking. The whiskey was good but the beer left a great deal to long for.

(Richard) What did they do when they were not fighting?

(Voice) wrote letters, sang songs and joked around. I didn't see any Hookers around where I was but there was talk. There was a whore house named Mary Jane's up the River that seemed popular.

(Richard) What did you like about traveling back?

(Voice) I wasn't a wanted man there—No one was trying to find me and bring me in. I could do what I wanted—within reason. There was a war but there was also an excitement because everyone felt the siege was almost over. No one was fool enough to think the war was done—this battle was a part of it, an important part.

(Richard) Still planning on going back to the past to hide?

(Voice) You want to come back? If you had a chance to go back in time where would you go?

(Richard) I have given it a great deal of thought. I think I would go back to Hollywood in the 1920s. There were great opportunities in the height of the Silent Era. It would be great to meet Mack Sennett the silent comedy director who might be a distant relative of mine.

(Voice) An interesting choice. I would select a more modern era— one with air conditioning at least.

(Richard) I should miss that.

(Voice) Maybe you shall get your wish.

(Richard) What do you mean?

(Voice) Are you up for a bit of time travel? Just an hour of so into the past?

(Richard) Just to visit?

(Voice) Yes, Yes. (Somehow I grew suspicious due to his tone.)

(Richard) But, first we must meet face too face.

(Voice) On November 21st you and your wife took a walk. Don't say anything. You rested on a bench. Do you recall the spot? We will meet there at 9:00 pm at night tomorrow. You know where I mean?

(Richard) Yes…I remember…

(Voice) Don't say any more. You had a cat in Ventura that ate spaghetti – I will ask his name. Don't say the name –this phone may well be tapped.
Now don't tell a soul. I got to go now—till tomorrow.

At that the phone went dead once again. A trip back in time sounds all rather exciting but, did I really want to go? I might be trapped back there. It would be a good place to hide someone. I had to shake

my head. I was starting to believe in the idea of time travel. All I had was the word of some voice on the phone. It could all be a joke of some sort—a scam bigger than anything that came out of Nigeria. The next thing he will be asking me for a bag of money and vanish into the night. I would wait and see what happened when we meet. It was a little like meeting deep throat. The place I sat down was at a little league baseball diamond not far from my house. How he had known this I don't know. Still. There are many homes not far from there and the mysterious Mullet Man might be someone who lived close at hand and may have been watching me.
I should be on my guard. I resolved to tell my wife what was up just incase something happened. I would be ready.

I got the feeling that something important was about to happen.

The Meeting

I started walking at 8:30. It was dark as pitch out. I had a handy flashlight with me. Something a ghost hunter never leaves home without. I also had a mini tape recorder and a notebook and pens, as well as my cell phone. My wife knew where I was going but my daughter Megan didn't. It was cold out I recall. I went down Santa Ana Street and cut over to the bike trail. It lead to the Little League Field.

I Kept an eye open for anyone who might be following. I was looking for strange vehicles as well. Only a few passed me and none seemed interested in me. Once I got onto the bike trail it was better, no bikes were using the narrow road and I used the flashlight. I was both excited and a bit leery. I told myself that the odds were 50-50 that he wouldn't show up. He would call with a story of some sort. I

Heard a dog bark and it set off a string of barking animals from the houses near the bike path. I looked into the gloom and made sure, once again that I wasn't being followed.

I vowed to stay 30 minutes and if nothing happened I would go home.   There was no game tonight at the field and I found the bench. I half expected to see the man waiting for me but I was quite alone. I sat down. The bench was cold. I glanced around to see if there were any microphones or bugs around. I saw nothing out of the ordinary and I doubted that I could even identify a modern bugging devise even if I found one.   I say back and started to review the whole story. A voice that seemed to know a great deal about me had been making wild claims that he was a time traveler with a door to the past and future. Some of the ideas made sense and others did not. The world of the future seemed a dark and fascist place where American Freedoms had almost vanished. It was a place of wars and destruction, ruined, radioactive cities and battles in far away lands. The world was nothing like the images pictured in fantasy—no star trek type world unity, no utopias, no flying cars.

I checked the dial of my illuminated watch. It was 9:03 now. My mysterious visitor was late.   I kept my eyes open to see if anyone was walking down the bike path towards me. There was nothing there. It seemed to grow colder but then maybe that was just my over imagination.

I saw a bright light from round a small building where they served hot dogs during the games. A figure stepped out. The form was wearing a tan sweatshirt with a hood. The hood was up and he work sweat pants and running shoes. He was thin. I couldn't see his face, He walked up to me and when he spoke I I dentified the voice.

(Voice) Good evening (he spoke slowly)

(Richard) Mr. Mullet Man I presume? (I extended my hand in friendship)

(Voice) Mr. Richard Senate I presume?

(Richard) Guilty as Charged. (He refused my handshake and sat down next to me).

(Voice) What was the name of you cat?

(Richard) My Cat?

(Voice) the one who ate spaghetti. The one you had years ago.

(Richard) Yes, It was Boris.

(Voice) Bingo. You really are Richard Senate.

(Richard) At last we meet. I must confess was expecting someone older. What are you 23 or 25?

(Voice) I am older than I look.

(Richard) You are the inventor of the time machine?

(Voice) None other. It took me five years to work it out. It was simple really.

(Richard) You were the one who placed the add in the newspaper?

(Voice) Overall, that was a mistake. It was after that that my problems all started.

(Richard) You live in Oak View?

(Voice) I lived in Oak View, but no longer. I can't say where I live now. It would not be safe.

(Richard) You say they are closing in on you?

(Voice) I will be forced to move on soon—sooner than I expected. I have used the time portal to gain advantages in the market and the winning numbers of the Lotto. Some of the winners were friends of mine. I needed the cash to continue the cat and mouse game.

(Richard) I could see that having a time machine could be a real asset. Why not go back to 9-10 and warn people about the world trade center?

(Voice) No one would believe me. I don't have much time and we could talk about what I should and should not have done all night. Believe me I have done that with some of my friends in the past and a few are still alive. I came here to give you something.

(Richard) What do you have? Do you have some evidence of your time journeys?

(Voice) As I promised you. In my trip to Santa Monica I made notes on the future. (He pulled out a hand full of papers, folded into quarters roughly)

(Richard) What do you expect me to do with these?

(Voice) Publish them in your book. I know you are writing one just as I know you are recording this conversation.

(Richard) I told you I would write up our conversations. That was part of the deal we made.

(Voice) Well, you don't need to worry about royalties, I don't need them. You couldn't send them to me anyway. In less you could go back to 1951 Encino.
I have been saving money up posing as an eccentric collector changing money back to bills and coins all printed and minted before 1950. I have several hundred thousand now and enough stock tips to keep me rich for the rest of my life.

(Richard) What about your time machine? All of your research?

(Voice) I will destroy every bit of it as I have all of my papers and notes. Except for these. (he waved the packet of papers before my face).

(Richard) What about future time trips?

(Voice) I will transfer much to my new home in Encino. I will tell people I'm an inventor. That might explain my wealth and my odd experiments. I have fake papers ready—The forgeries cost me a mint, but people were not so suspicious in the 1950s.

(Richard) When are you leaving?

(Voice) Soon, very soon. I will let you know when I go. Have you made up your mind about going back with me?

(Richard) Tempting offer but I couldn't leave….

(Voice) I know, I know, your wife and family. We be happy. I had other plans but the time line is closing in on me. I wanted to take you on a trip… but its not to be.
(Richard) I understand (I didn't believe he would anyway).

(Voice) Here are the papers. Promise me you will burn them after you transcribe them. The forces against me might use them to secure my DNA.

(Richard) Should I eat them? This sounds like a bad spy movie.

(Voice) promise me you will burn them.

(Richard) OK I will. (At that he handed me the packet and stood up)

(Voice) I must go, (He looked at a strange wrist watch that seemed as large as a cell phone with a glowing display of numbers).

(Richard) Will we meet again?

(Voice) Perhaps. (He nodded his head and almost silently ran back towards the building. He dashed around the side where I could not see him and their was a bright flash of light—then all was still save for the dogs barking).

I felt the papers in my hand. They were slick and were maybe ten inches square. They had pastel on the edges and they were covered in small printed letters like a draftsman uses on a blue print. Most were capitals. The light was too dim to read them and I didn't turn on the flash light. I got up shaking as a shiver raced down my spine. Had he used the time machine to leave? What was that flash? It was a bit like the flash of a camera. I could well have been a trick of some sort. One thing was clear. The man didn't look much like the pictures of Mullet Man I had seen. I walked back slowly trying to drink in every word. I had tried to tape the conversation but the battery in the small tape recorder was drained and it recorded almost nothing.

The Eighth Call

Two days later the phone rang at 9:00. My wife and daughter were gone. I was about to leave the house. I knew who it was before I head the familiar voice.

(Voice) Do you have a moment? I need to talk.

(Richard) Yes, what is it about? I read the papers you left.

(Voice) I wish I could have researched more for you about the future. Maybe it can be changed. It was good to see you in your modern form.

(Richard) What do you mean?
(Voice) I have seen you in the past, I must say you need to lose weight.

(Richard) How can I believe you?

(Voice) Trust me. I don't have much time. They are getting better each day and I can't keep hiding out, I was in a cabin in Rose Valley area for a time. Then I was in a big house in Ventura off Ocean

Avenue. I thought I was safe there. I am going to have to move again.

(Richard) Was this why you called? (I figured this was where he would ask for money—to move).

(Voice) To warn you, that's all. They may come or call you in the next few days. Don't tell them anything. When I am safe again, I will contact you again.

(Richard) How long will you be moving?

(Voice) I don't know. It all depends. You have a good soul my friend. I will contact you before I escape back into the past.
(At that he rudely hung up.)

I didn't hear from the man for two more weeks. When his has call came it was almost anti-climatic. In the time I received no calls or had any strange visitors. Late at night my trash can was upended and ransacked. But was it a homeless man looking for goods to sell or a kid doing a prank, I shall never know.

The Last Call

The phone rang at 9:30—at least that's what my notes say. Somehow I knew this was different. Maybe it was a psychic thing or just a hunch. I picked it up and heard the distinct voice once again.

(Voice) Hello Richard. How are you?

(Richard) I'm fine, how are you.

(Voice) Not well my friend. I will be leaving soon, in a few hours in fact. I have gotten rid of any trace of me here in the Ojai Valley.

(Richard) Then this is your last contact?

(Voice) Yes, I am sad to say that things have changed in the last few weeks that render it impossible for me to stay. I had plans to do so much more. Time travel is very taxing on the body, I have found, and the constant security is something that builds up.

(Richard) I guess its all very stressful.

(Voice) You don't know the half of it. There is so much I wanted to tell you but never got the chance. I do know one thing, man shouldn't travel in time, its not something we should do even if we have the means. Aristotle once wrote something on a magic ring. A guy finds a ring and it can make him invisible. He uses it to become rich but it corrupts him and he loses his soul. Time travel is a bit like that.

(Richard) Where will you go?

(Voice) Into the past—I will not say where or when. But it will not be too far back. Maybe the 60s, maybe the 50s. I will move out of the area. Florida maybe or Texas, I don't want to stay in California.

(Richard) Will you keep your Time Machine?

(Voice) I don't know. I may return to see you sometime in the future. I may not.
The things I need to keep it running may not exist in the past.

(Richard) All you need is electricity, right?

(Voice) No, there are other things that I need to keep it up. I will use it sparingly if I continue to use it at all.

(Richard) Then this is good bye?

(Voice) Yes. I promised you I would call before I left. I will see you again in the past. If you a stranger walking up to you as a child and hands you a $100 bill it will be me.

(Richard) I will think your some sort of nut or a pervert.

(Voice) I may do it in a different way, like offer you a great job or give a job to your Dad. It will be like "good luck."

(Richard) I don't recall anything like that now, at least not that I can recall.

(Voice) Why? Because the deed hasn't happened yet. I have grown quite fond of you over the last few months. You are one of the few honest people I have met. I wish you well.

(Richard) Good luck in all you do. May you find the peace you are looking for in the past.

(Voice) I must go now, Time is running out. I have a bag of things I will be talking back with me this time that should make my life comfortable.

(Richard) *Via Con Dios.* Good journey.

(Voice) Good Bye. (At that he hung up)

Postscript

About an hour later there was a power failure in Oak View. When the lights went out I had to smile. It was just the Mullet Man traveling to a new place in time. I knew I would miss him. I half believed his story, yet another part of me thought I was the victim of some elaborate hoax. Was the Mullet Man real or some young man's fantasy? Maybe I will know for sure if I wake one day with the memory of a stranger handing me a hundred dollar bill back in 1959. So far, I have no memory of a strange benefactor.

I present the facts to you so that you can make the final judgment. Ultimately, time will tell if the bleak world of the future he described is true or false. Only, in the future will we know if Mullet Man was the greatest scam artist to walk California or if he was an unknown genius forced to flee by the workings of an unfeeling and intrusive government. I always wonder what he had in his bag he took away with him? Was it stock tips or some new invention? I don't know, but what ever he took would make him wealthy and perhaps powerful. What would you take back with you? I present the facts as best I remember them to you. I may have left out a few details only out of respect for the stranger who called with visions of the future. Where ever you are, and if you read these words, I must thank you and wish you well.

"Mullet Man" in the Civil War

APENDIX

From the notes of the Mullet Man made in the future. Interpret them as you wish.

2017 Second Mexican Revolution, more civil war that revolution, starts in Northern Mexico. 19 million flee to USA. US supports Mexican Government.

2019 Washington D.C. lost to terrorists flying a Nuke Bomb into White House on August 19, Dirty Bomb Wind carry fallout. Baltimore hit. Downtown Richmond VA hit by blast.
1 million die in first 10 days, In weeks after, 1.5 to 2 million die in six months after blast due to radiation sickness.

2019 Secretary of State was in London. He becomes president of US. He orders attack on Saudi Arabia. Three cities nuked in 30 minutes.

2019 September , US capital Moved to New York City.

2019 Two Western Canadian Provinces join USA. The 52 and 53rd states.

2020 North American Union formed. Rest of Canada joins, except Quebec,

2020 New Flag selected November 18, Union day.

2021 The Republic of Cuba joins the North American Union.

2021 End of Second Mexican Revolution, the peace of Nuevo Leon.

2022 September 16, Mexico Joins North American Union.

2023 New Capital built at Bolder, Colorado.

2026 – 2027 Ebola Pandemic (called E-Boy) hits the world. 1 billion perish. NAU lost 72 million many perish in Mexico.

2026 Jamaica, hit hard by E-Boy, joins NAU

2027 Quebec Joins NAU along with Haiti and Costa Rica.

2028   War with China over Southeast Asia and Panama. 1.2 million perish when war turns nuclear after attack on San Diego.

Los Angeles/Burbank lost, Pearl Harbor Lost. Attacks on Seattle and San Francisco thwarted. War lasts 50 days. Shanghai, Hong Kong, Beijing destroyed. The naval battle of the China Sea a draw. Japan neutral.

2028 War between South African Union and United Arab Union. Cairo falls to South Africa.

2029 European Union declares war on South Africa, Invades Morocco.

2030 Europeans defeated at Tunis in massive robot tank battle.

2031 NAU joins EUA in war on South Africa. Liberia joins NAU.

2032 Allies invade Congo and Morocco. South Africa defeated in North Africa.

2033 Naval Battle at Cape Town. South Africa defeated at sea.

2034 South African War ends. Dictator takes his own life. Republic Formed.

2035 First city formed on the moon.

2035 All Central America Now part of the NAU.

2036 Bahamas Joins the EUA along with Bermuda.

2037 New planet discovered outside solar system by EUA with life.

2037 Russian Confederation joins EUA. ❧❧❧❧❧❧❧